Copyright

compil

E.C. "Red" Stangland

POLISH & Other ETHNIC JOKES

published by

NORSE PRESS

909 E. 35th St.

Sioux Falls, S. Dak. 57105 U.S.A.

Illustrated by Don Steinbeck

ISBN 0-9602692-1-5

Q: Two Italians, one fat, one thin, fall off a tall building. Which lights first?

A: Who cares?

A Pole marries a Puerto Rican and they have a child. Named it "Retardo."

Patrick the Irishman let it be known around the neighborhood that he had become a diamond cutter. Later, the neighbors found out that he mowed grass at the ball park.

A guy was half Polish and half Japanese. He made calculators that don't work.

Customer: "Waiter, you've got your thumb on my steak!"

Italian Waiter: "Sorry sir...I didn't want it to fall on the floor again."

An Iranian firing squad was about to execute two Irishmen. When asked if they had any last words, Pat launched into a denunciation of his captors, calling them terrible names. His mate, Casey, leaned over to whisper, "Pat, don't make trouble."

Stage manager: So you wish to see Ming Ling, the great Chinese wrestler?

Lady: Yes, tell him his mother is here from Israel.

A Polish girl walks into a bar with a duck under her arm.
Bartender: You can't come in here with a pig.
Girl: This ain't a pig...it's a duck.
Bartender: I wasn't talking to you...I was talking to the duck.

Irishman: Do you talk to your wife when you make love?
Italian: Sometimes...if I happen to be near a phone.

A guy is giving his girl a ride on a motorcycle. She has her leather jacket on backwards for extra warmth. They hit a truck and land on the pavement. A Pole stops to be of assistance. A cop shows up and notes that both cyclists are dead. The Pole tells the cop: "Well, he was dead right away, but she showed signs of life until I twisted her head around to the front where it belongs."

Eye Doctor: "Have your eyes ever been checked?"
Polack: "No...they've always been blue."

A Norwegian, an Irishman and a German were sentenced to be electrocuted. First, the Irishman was strapped in the chair and the switch was pushed. Nothing happened, so the Irishman was freed. Same thing happened to the German. As the Norwegian was led into the execution room, the prison guard remarked, "Sure has been a lucky day for those two guys." Said the Norwegian, "Vell, I should say so, becoss I can see the plug has come out of the socket under the chair."

Ever wonder how the Grand Canyon was formed? A Scotchman dropped a nickel down a gopher hole.

A Swede had trouble putting "Happy Birthday" on a cake. His main problem was getting the cake in the typewriter.

Why do Italians always talk with their hands? Because of the garlic, they can't stand each other's breath.

The nurse told the German to strip to the waist. So he took off his pants.

The Pole called on his girl friend and his shirt was dripping wet. When asked why he replied, "The label said 'Wash and Wear.' "

A lazy Italian hold up man called up a bank: "This is a stickup. Send me $50,000."

A Pole declined a street peddler's attempt to sell him pornographic pictures. Said the Pole, "I don't even own a pornograph."

Did you hear about the Polack who...Wouldn't go out with his wife because she was a married woman?

Thought "No kidding" meant birth control?

Called his girl Tapioca because she could be made in a minute?

Took his pregnant wife to the supermarket because they advertised free delivery?

Put iodine on his paycheck after he received a cut in pay?

Thought that asphalt was a hemorrhoid problem?

What's the big deal about split level houses? Thirty years ago if you lived over a garage, you had to be Italian.

A Rent-a-car company was all set to blanket Poland with an advertising campaign, only to discover that Poland has no roads.

Why don't Polacks watch Johnny Carson?
Because none of them can stay sober past 10:30.

How do you identify a Polish intellectual?
When you see one not moving his lips while reading.

A Norwegian called his wife "Crisco" because she's fat in the can.

How can Swedes distinguish boy sardines from girl sardines?
They watch to see which can they come out of.

Why does it take three Polacks to eat a rabbit?
Because it requires two just to look out for cars.

Famous inventions: The Poles invented the toilet seat. Twenty years later, the Italians invented the hole in it.

Why don't the Swedes tell Polish jokes?
——Because they don't understand them.

A Bohemian decided to drive to Omaha to see his cousin. About 20 miles from his destination, he saw a sign, "OMAHA LEFT." So he turned around and went back home.

Why don't Polish mothers nurse their babies?
——Because it is so painful when they boil the nipple.

Two Swedes were talking in the park when a bird splattered one of them on the head. Eyeing the mess, the victim's companion offered to go get some toilet paper. "Von't do no good," said the messed-up one, "by the time you get back, dat bird will be four miles avay."

Woman: I was just raped by a Pole.
Policeman: How do you know he was Polish?
Woman: I had to show him how.

A Swede came home one day and shot his dog. When a neighbor expressed surprise, the Swede explained, "Some vun phoned me up and said my vife vas fooling around vith my best friend."

Why do Bohemians smile when it lightnings?
They think they're getting their picture taken.

Ever wonder who invented streaking?. It was a Swede who mistook Ben Gay for Preparation H.

The Polish government has been having problems with their space program. Their astronaut keeps falling off the kite.

A Pole appeared with five other men in a rape case police line-up. As the victim entered the room, the Pole blurted, "Yep...that's her!

Irishman: (In a cemetery) "Why did you die? Oh, WHY did you die?
Polack: You really feel bad. Close relative?
Irishman: No. My wife's first husband. WHY DID YOU DIE?"

Two Swedes brought their wives on a trip to America. They were soon trying to adopt American customs...in fact, Lars even suggested to Ole that they swap partners "like they do in America." So they did. About 11:30 that night, Lars said to Ole..."I vonder how da vimmen folks are getting along."

Why does it take two Polacks to make chocolate chip cookies?
One to mix the batter and one to squeeze the rabbit.

How do Polacks re-cycle toilet paper?
They send it to Mr. Whipple who squeezes the you-know-what out of it.

The Bohemians have invented a new parachute.
Opens on impact.

Why do Polish dogs have flat noses?
From chasing parked cars.

A German decided to get a vasectomy because he didn't want any more grandchildren.

There once was a Irish Kamakaze pilot who managed to rack up 25 suicide missions.

During the big flood around Fargo in 1975, several Norwegians waited by the river bank with toothbrushes. They were waiting for the Crest.

A—Polish Sex Manual
B—Polish Weather Report
(tree below zero)
C—Polish Quarter Pounder

Polack Tying His Shoe

FOR SALE·

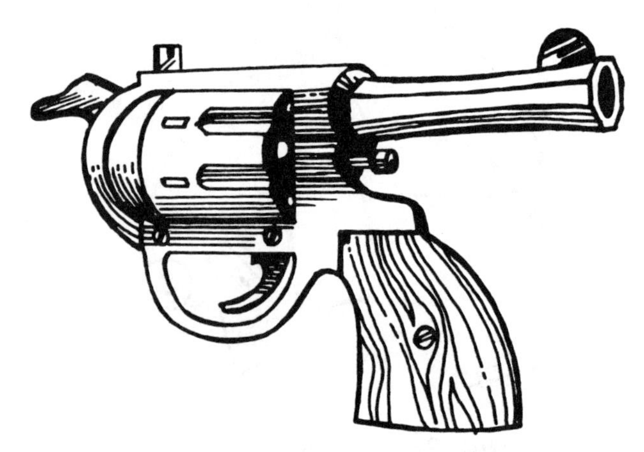

Polish pistol (used only once)

Two Norwegians Walking Abreast

Did you hear about the Finlander who had his bathroom carpeted?
He liked it so well that he had it carpeted all the way to the house.

A Polish lady quit using the pill.
Kept falling out.

Lady (attending the Olympics): "Are you a Pole Vaulter?"
Norwegian: "No . . . I'm a Norwegian . . . and my name ain't Valter."

A TV network is planning a two hour special. A Swede will attempt to count to 100.

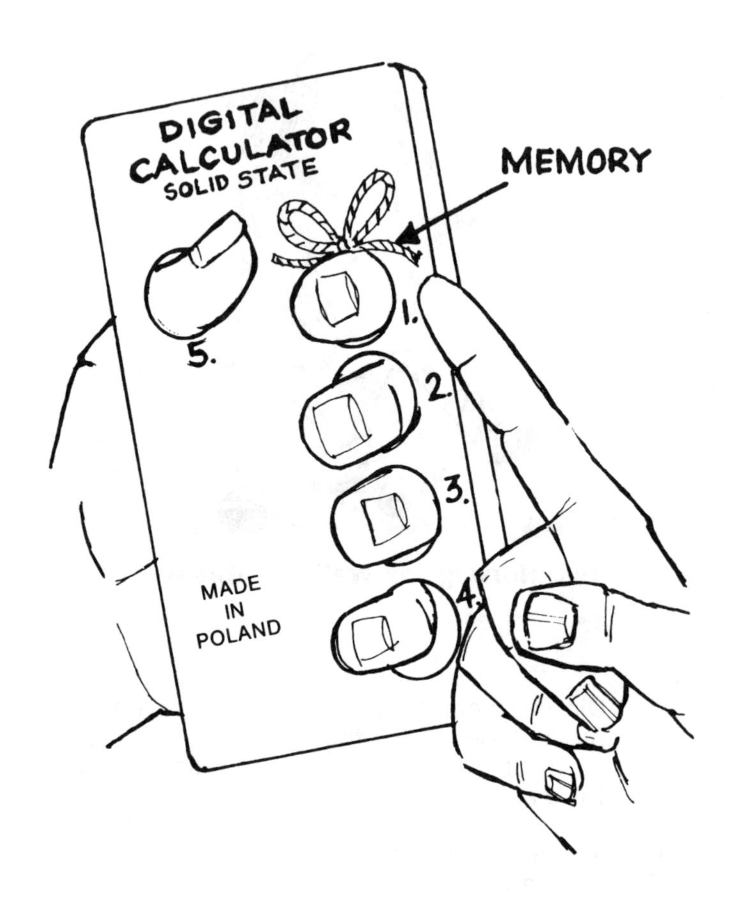

Here's a Swedish Wedding announcement:

C2DV

L Mr

(Translation: "Come to da vedding; Lena mister period").

Woman: Oh, my goodness...my husband is driving in the driveway!
Irishman: I better get outta here. Where is your back door?
Woman: We don't have a back door.
Irishman: Well, where would you like one?

Did you hear about the intelligent Swede?
It was just a rumor.

An Irishman was hired to paint the center stripe down the middle of a new highway. The first day he completed 3 miles, two miles the second day, but only one the 3rd day. Noting the difference, the superintendent asked for an explanation. "I dunno," puzzled the Irishman. "I guess it just kept getting farther to go back to that can of paint."

What did they call the Polack who was half Indian?
"Running Dummy."

A Norwegian entered a lumber yard and asked for some 4 by 2's. "We don't have 4 by 2's, but we DO have 2 by 4's." "Vell, dat's OK," said the Norsky. "How long do you want them," queried the lumberman. "Vell, quite a while," answered the Norwegian..."Ve're planning to build a barn."

We know a Polack who thinks a Sanitary Belt is booze from a clean shot glass.

Crop scientists have come up with a new strain known as "Swedish Oats."
They are tall, light colored and empty headed.

The Italians are proud of their new zoo.
They built a fence around Yugoslavia.

Ole calls Lena his "Melancholy Baby" because she has a head like a melon and a face like a Collie.

A German was brought to the hospital with severe facial burns. Seems he had been bobbing for French Fries.

Two Swedes were trying to train their Bird Dog. Said Nels; "Trow him up yust vunce more, Ole; an' if he don't fly dis time, yust shoot him."

I love to watch the Polish National Symphony between selections when they empty the saliva from their instruments. What's funny is that it's a string orchestra.

Italian Girl: "How come you're so popular with the men?"

Polish Girl: "I give up."

The Polish air force hopes to soon have a squadron of jets in the air...just as soon as they obtain a large enough supply of cobs for fuel.

A Pole moved to Ireland and joined the IRA. His first assignment was to blow up a bus. But he failed because he burned his mouth on the exhaust pipe.

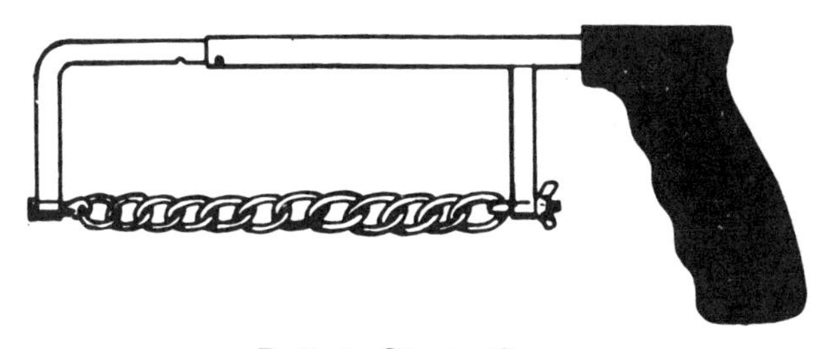

Polish Chain Saw

A Finlander decided to take up hunting. So, off into the woods he went...when suddenly a beautiful blonde appeared. "Are you game?" asked the Finn. "I certainly am," purred the blonde. So the Finlander shot her.

The wealthy Jewish lady was regaling her Haddassah club members with her latest travels. "Yaass," she remarked, "this summer Herschel and I went around the world. Next year . . . I suppose we'll go somewhere else."

A Polack inherited a penguin and his neighbor noticed the Pole walking the penguin in his backyard. "I just inherited this penguin," said the Pole, "What do you think I should do with him?" "If I were you," said the neighbor, "I'd take him to the zoo." Next day, the neighbor noticed the Polack with the penguin in his backyard. "Hey," he called, "didn't you take that penguin to the zoo?" "Sure," said the Pole, "and tomorrow I'm taking him to the ball game."

Did you hear about the Bohemian who could count to 10?
No?
Would you believe FIVE?

A Polack went on an elephant hunt, but was forced to turn back because he developed a hernia from carrying the decoy.

Sandy McTavish, a true and thrifty Scotchman, in a burst of generosity decided to give his wife a mink set for her birthday. A trap and a rifle.

Dane (sniffing): Did you take a bath, Ole?
Norwegian: No. Is one missing?

Italian: Have an accident?
Pole (in battered condition): No thanks. Just had one.

Danny O'Rourke was having trouble getting his car started. He finally lost his Irish temper and commenced a tirade that contained not a few oaths and obscenities. Father Murphy happened along and remonstrated with O'Rourke. "Now Danny, me boy, why don't you just pray over the situation instead of all that cursing?"

You go ahead and pray," said Danny. So the good Father prayed for three minutes, stepped into the car, turned the key...and it started.

"Well, I'll be damned," said Father Murphy in amazement.

A Polish girl considered getting an abortion because she didn't think the baby was hers.

How do they brain wash a (Ethnic of your choice)
Answer: Give 'em an enema.

Two Danes just arrived in the U.S. encountered their first hot dog stand. Knute examined the interior of his hot dog and asked his companion, "Jens, what part of the dog did YOU get?"

An Italian lady with 10 kids had been listening to the latest Papal encyclical on birth control. So she sat down and wrote the following letter: "Dear Mr. Pope: if you don'-a play-a da game, no make-a da rules."

If a Polack throws a pin at you, what is the best thing to do?
Run like hell because chances are he'll be holding a hand grenade in his mouth.

A Pole walked into the post office and noticed a poster that read, "Man wanted for robbing a bank in Chicago." So he inquired as to where he should apply for the job.

A Finlander went to his Doctor for a physical, complaining about his sex life. The Doc told him to walk ten miles a day, then call him on the phone. A week later, the Finlander telephoned his Doctor. "How's your sex life," inquired the Doc. "What sex?" blurted the Finlander."I'm seventy miles from home."

A Jewish lady on the streetcar kept looking a well dressed man up and down, asking him if he was Jewish. He kept denying it, until finally in exasperation he snorted, "Okay, lady, if it'll make you happy, I'm Jewish."

"Hmmmph," she hmmped, "You don't look Jewish."

A young lad from a well to do Jewish family was assigned to write an essay in school on the subject of poverty. Here's what he wrote: "Once upon a time there was a poor family. The father was poor; the mother was poor; the children were poor; and even the maid and butler were poor."

Back in the depression days, beefsteak was 8 cents a pound. Ike was serving a customer and weighed up eight pounds with the following mathematics: "Eight times eight is eighty-eight...but for you, since I like you, I'll give it to you for eighty cents."

Rachel: "I was to Doctor Horowitz today...and what a thrill! He said he had never seen such a perfect body."

Max: "What did he say about your fat ass?"

Rachel: "Funny thing...he didn't even mention you."

Cohen: I just collected $50,000 flood insurance.

Goldfarb: How do you start a flood?

Stein and Wasserman stood by the coffin of their partner, Gold. Wiping a tear from his eye, Stein impulsively reached for his wallet and placed $500 in currency in the coffin, remarking, "Max liked money...he would have appreciated this token of our friendship." Wasserman, not to be outdone, said, "I, too, would like to place $500 in the bier of our dear departed friend and partner. Since I don't have any cash on me, I will write out a check for $1,000." Whereupon, Wasserman reached for and pocketed the $500 cash.

Stash: My cousin once worked in the circus, putting his right hand in the lion's mouth.

Stan: What cousin was that?

Stash: My cousin Lefty.

Why is it that Christ could not have been born in Poland?

It would have been impossible to find three wise men.

There's a rumor that the Italians are making a deal with the Hilton Hotel chain to take over the Leaning Tower of Pisa...in which case they could call it the "Tiltin' Hilton." If that didn't work out, they could always turn in into a Pizza Parlor and call it the "Leaning Tower of Pizza."

Mrs. Baum was trying out a fency-shmency Jewish restaurant. As she studied the menu, she noticed the waiter scratching himself. "You have hemorrhoids?" she inquired. Without batting an eyelash, the waiter answered, "Madam, only what's on the menu."

A tourist from the mainland was seeing the sights of Hawaii. He spotted a Rabbi and stepped up to ask, "Sir, is it correct to say 'Hawaii' or 'Havaii?' Answered the Rabbi, "Havaii," "Thank you, Sir," said the tourist, "By the way how long have you been over here?" "Two veeks," said the Rabbi.

Yenta, a shapely young Jewish lady, stopped in a fabric store and ordered 14 yards of flannel. "For a nightgown," she explained. "What! 14 yards of flannel for ONE nightgown?" Yenta smiled and blushed as she whispered in the clerk's ear, "My husband, Hyman is past 70. And frankly, he gets a bigger kick out of looking for it than finding it."

Mrs. Greenbaum drove a beautiful new Cadillac to the used car lot and offered to sell it for $50. The dealer was all shook up, figuring something HAD to be wrong with it. He just couldn't make up his mind to accept the offer...so Mrs. Greenbaum decided to explain. "Well, my late husband, God rest his soul, died two weeks ago. I happen to know he had been having an affair with his secretary. And in his Will he mentioned his secretary should have the proceeds from selling his new $24,000 Cadillac."

Two Jewish kids were trying to outbrag each other. "Listen," said Izzy. "My aunt is such a great singer. One night she got up to high C and she held it for three minutes."

"You should talk," said little Ike. "My aunt...she got up to P one night...and someone was in the bathroom so she held it for an hour and a half."

Katz: Did you know that Columbus was Jewish?

Blum: How so?

Katz: Don't you remember how he kept saying, "Sale on...sale on?"

There's a nasty rumor that spare parts from a Jewish "bris" are sent over to Ireland to be made into cops.

Ancient Jewish Proverb: "Whether you're rich or poor...it's nice to have money."

How do you recognize a Polish airliner?

Look carefully and you'll see hair under the wings.

The Bohemian tried with all his might to quit smoking. He finally succeeded by substituting chewing toothpicks for smoking cigarettes. But, alas, six months later he died from Dutch Elm disease.

The winner in the Miss Poland contest had quite a figure...a perfect 38.

38-38-38.

A Jewish gentleman named Max came home one day and was horrified to discover his best friend, Meyer, hiding in the closet without so much as a stitch of clothing on. "Meyer, my friend," he moaned, "YOU . . . of all people, having an affair with my wife. YOU . . . after I brought you over from Germany and saved your life . . . after I bought you clothes, gave you food, found you a job. Why? Tell me why, Meyer . . . after all I've done for you?"

"Nu?" shrugged Meyer, "So what have you done for me lately?"

A Jewish father was dying and his children gathered at his bedside. The eldest, Morris, spoke in hushed tones, "Papa...tell us...where would you like to be buried...here in California or back in New York." Papa opened his eyes slightly and with great effort answered, "Surprise me."

Two Danes at the funeral of their friend Nels. "He sure looks good," said one. "He should," remarked the other, "he yust got out of the hospital."

Know why the Swede ate beans on Friday? So he could have a bubble bath on Saturday.

"Why do Polacks have such pretty noses?" Because they're hand picked.

Two Irishmen were trying to get a mule into the barn but its ears were too long. One Irishman suggested raising the barn. The other one thought they should dig a trench. "No, you dummy," exploded the first, "it's the ears that are too long, not the legs."

"How does a Pole grease his car?"

He goes out and runs over an Italian.

A great medical breakthrough was recently reported. The Danes have now performed the first successful hernia transplant.

1st Norsky: What's in the sack?
2nd Norsky: Chickens.
1st Norsky: How many?
2nd Norsky: If you can guess, I'll give you both of dem.

"Who invented the Limbo?"

A Polack trying to sneak under a pay toilet door.

A Bohemian's wife had triplets...so he went out looking for the other two guys.

We heard of a Pole who was so dumb he thought "Innuendo" was the Italian word for Preparation H.

"What has an IQ of 104?"

Six Polacks.

A Bohemian had a tough job sweeping up after the circus elephants. When asked why he didn't quit, he exclaimed, "What, and leave Show Biz?"

1st Swede: My brother's got a case of hemorrhoids.
2nd Swede: Svell, Let's go over and help him drink it.

Street Evangelist: "How would you like to be a Jehovah's witness?"
Swede: "Heck, I didn't even see the accident."

A Finlander arrive in California two weeks late on his trip from Duluth. He explained the delay: "Vell, I kept seeing those signs, 'Clean Rest Rooms' so I had to clean 400 on the way out."

1st Swede: "I stuck up for you the other day."

2nd Swede: "You did?"

1st Swede: "Yah...someone said you vasn't fit to sleep with the pigs. And I said you vas."

Why don't Polacks swat flies?

It's their national bird.

What happened when the Polish library burned to the ground?

Both books were destroyed and one hadn't even been colored in.

Who was the dumbest Swede?

The one who thought Einstein was "one beer."

What are the three shortest books?
1. Book of Italian victories in WW II.
2. Irish book of etiquette.
3. Norwegian book of knowledge.

What did the Dane call his cocktail of Vodka and Milk of Magnesia?

"A Phillips Screwdriver."

Swede reading the Bible for the first time: "It says a lot about St. Paul, but deres notting in it about Minnoplis."

Why don't they allow Polacks to swim in Lake Michigan?

Because they leave a ring.

Did you hear about the German who quit chainsmoking?

He said they were too hard to light.

Describe Bohemian matched luggage.

A pair of brown paper sacks.

It seems the Pole was having his eyes checked and the doctor pointed to the chart on the wall with all the ZXYQZZXX's on it.

Can you read the bottom line?" asked the Doctor.

"Read it?" answered the Pole.
" I know him personally."

A Norwegian on his first plane ride. The pilot announced one engine had quit and the flight would be delayed a half hour. Later, another engine went out, and the pilot announced a one-hour delay. When a third engine went dead, the pilot announced a 90-minute delay. "My goodness," exclaimed the Norwegian, "If that last engine qvits, ve'll be up here all night!"

What is this?

A Polish monogrammed handkerchief.

And these:

Polish silverware.

When the Swede accidentally lost 50 cents in the outhouse, he immediately threw in his watch and billfold. He explained, "I'm not going down dere just for 50 cents."

Two German brothers kept their two horses in a pasture. To tell them apart, they trimmed the tail on one horse. Later, they discovered the black horse was about 8 inches shorter than the white one.

Why is there always a garbage can present at a Norwegian wedding?

To keep the flies off the bride.

How can you recognize the bride at a Bohemian wedding?

She's the one wearing the white maternity dress.

A Polack received a pair of water skis for his birthday.
He went crazy looking for a hill on Lake Michigan.

What are some typical prizes at a Polish raffle?

2nd Prize: An all expense paid trip to Poland.

1st Prize: Seventy-five cents.

What was the tragedy concerning the four Polacks who drowned in the station wagon that went into the river?

The wagon could have held 6.

How can you identify a level headed Norwegian?

When the snoose runs out of both corners of his mouth.

Who won the Polish beauty contest?

Nobody.

Describe a Polish Toronado.

A '54 Chevy with snow tires on the front.

The Swedes in Minneapolis have come up with a new drink. They mix Tang and prune juice...and call it "Prune Tang."

Swede (working a crossword puzzle): What's a four-letter word ending in "it" for something that lies on the bottom of a bird cage.?

Norwegian: Grit.

Swede: Would you mind if I borrowed your eraser?

Q. What's pink, fuchsia, purple, lime, magenta, burgundy, and chartreuse?

A. The suit worn by Poland's best dressed man.

A Polish family moved to a new neighborhood. The kid of the family, little Stanislaus, watched the next door neighbor mow his lawn. "We be almost as good as you be," said Stan, "we got lawn mover like you." Next day, Stan spoke to the neighbor again: "We be JUST as good as you be. We got Cadillac like you." Two days later, the young Pole again addressed the neighbor: "We be better than you be." "Now just a minute, kid," exploded the neighbor, "First, you said you was almost as good. Then you said you was just as good. Now you say you're **better** than me. How do you figure?" Smirked Stanislaus, "We don't live next door to no Polacks."

A Norwegian answers the phone at 3 a.m. Wrong number, so the caller apologizes. "Dats OK," said the Norwegian, "I had to get up to answer the phone anyvay."

A Bohemian was strolling through the farm yard one day when he gazed down to find himself ankle deep in manure.

"Good heavens," he exclaimed, "I'm MELTING!"

Two Norwegians were building a house. One of them reached into a sack of nails and said, "Lars, you got us the wrong kind of nails. Dese nails have got the point on the wrong end."

"Dat's okay," said Lars, "Ve can use dem on the other side of the house."

Why does it take 5 Polacks to paint a house?

You need one to hold the brush and 4 to turn the house.

1st man: Do you know how to talk Polish?

2nd man: Nope...couldn't get the hang of it.

1st man: How does it feel to be DUMBER than a Polack?

A neighborhood bar had customers of many ethnic persuasions. The Russian would come in and order "VT." "That's easy," said the bartender. "Vodka Tonic." The Irishman would order "WW." "Okay," said the bartender, "I know that one, too. Whiskey and water." One day a Norwegian came in and ordered. "Give me a 15." "Fifteen," bellowed the bartender. "I know all the nicknames for drinks but I never heard of a '15'. What the devil is a '15'?"

Answered the Norwegian, "Seven and Seven."

A Swede and a Norwegian went up in a plane together. When the plane developed engine trouble, the two bailed out in parachutes. The Swede reached the ground in a matter of about a minute. But the Norwegian got lost and didn't get down until a half hour later.

A Bohemian was hired to operate an elevator. But he lost his job after the first day. Couldn't learn the route.

Several Swedish farmers from Minnesota, dissatisfied with low farm prices, decided to march on Washington. At last report, they were 15 miles south of Seattle.

A Bohemian came into town wearing just one overshoe. He said he heard on the radio there was a 50% chance of snow.

A Polack took a job with the Mafia. He was instructed to hi-jack a Jet. So he came back with Joe Namath.

On a Viking ship the Captain addressed the crew. "I've got some good news and some bad news. The good news is...you get to change underwear today. The bad news is ...Lars, you change with Ole. Ole...you change with Nels..."

Recently a Swede was seen with just one snow tire on his car. His reason: Winter was half over.

First gent: Say, how would you like to hear a Polish story?

Second gent: Hold it! I want to warn you that I'm Polish.

First Gent: Oh, well, in that case, I'll tell it real slow.

"Mission Impossible" is planning a special on TV. Going to try to give a Polack a bath.

How do you hide money from a Polack?

Place it under a soap dish.

Why does it only require two men to bury a Swede?

Because there are only two handles on a garbage can.

Two Santa Clauses up on the roof. Which one is Polish?

The one with the Easter basket.

How was Streaking invented?

When they tried to give a Polack a bath.

Describe a Swedish "Saint and Sinner."

A hot dog and a carp.

The Poles finally developed an SST (Supersonic Transport). During the attempted first flight, the plane stopped at the end of the runway, having run out of coal.

At a fancy party, how can you identify the Polack?

He's the one with the yellow tennis shoes and the rusty zipper.

A cop blew his whistle at the Bohemian motorist.

"Hey, you dummy...didn't you see the arrows?"

"Heck," answered the Bohemian, "I didn't even see the Indians."

What happened after the Swede lost a $50 bet on a TV football play?

He lost another $50 on the instant replay.

Describe a Polish pullman.

A box-car.

Who was the most famous Norwegian inventor?

Henry Fjord.

Who discovered Poland?

The Roto Rooter man.

A noted lawyer, B. Nels Simons was being served in a fancy restaurant. "Waiter," said Simons, "why is your finger in my soup?"

"I injured my finger today," said the waiter, "and my doctor said to keep it in a warm place."

"Well," snorted the lawyer, "why don't you put it where the sun don't shine?"

"I do," answered the waiter, "when I'm out in the kitchen."

What do you call a Norwegian who marries a moron?
A social climber.

Do Polish teachers have ESP?

Yes. Extra simple pupils.

At a Cannibal market, brains were considered a delicacy.

Of all the brains on sale, the Polish brains were priced the highest. The merchant explained, "Never been used."

Two Irishmen went deer hunting when one of them accidentally shot the other.

The victim was finally taken to a hospital where the Doctors labored to save him.

As the other Irishman paced out in the lobby, the Doctor came out and said, "He was pretty badly shot...but I think we might have been able to save him if you hadn't dressed him out."

Why does it take 3 Swedes to replace a light bulb?

Because it requires one to hold the bulb and two to turn the ladder.

What's black and blue and lies on the sidewalk?

The guy who tells too many ethnic stories.

Two Norwegians noticed two men fishing in the middle of a plowed field.

"Why don't ve go and tell dem dey von't catch anything out dere?" remarked one.

"No use," said the other, "ve don't got a boat."

What do you say about an Irishman who has a warm outhouse and a cold six-pack of beer?

---He's living in the fast lane.

A Cannibal was checking out prices at his local meat market.

He asked the vendor why the Irishman cost 90¢ a pound, the German 85¢ a pound and the Norwegian was priced $1.50 per pound.

"Why does the Norwegian cost so much," he asked.

"Well," came the answer, "did you ever try to **clean** one?"

Did you hear about the Polack who broke his shoulder during a milk drinking contest?

A cow fell on him.

Why are Poles allowed only 15 minutes for lunch break?

Any longer and they'd have to be retrained.

Describe a Swedish garbage disposal.

A pig under the sink.

Recently a Polish country & western singer got herpes of the eyes. Seems he'd been "Looking for Love in all the wrong places."

Where do you look for Polish obituaries?

Under "home improvements."

What did the Polack do with the Gold Medal he won at the Olympics?

He was so proud of it, he had it bronzed.

What caused the drowning of four Bohemians recently?

They tried to highjack a bus to Cuba.

Define: "Dope ring."

Six Polacks in a circle.

Then we heard about the Bohemian who cut down a big grove of trees with a chain saw. When he got through, someone showed him how to start the engine.

Al: How many Polacks does it take to roof a house?

Pal: I give up. How many?

Al: All depends on how thin you slice them.

A Norwegian, recently arrived in the U.S., was showing off his knowledge of the months of the year in English: "Yoon, You-lie, All-guts, split timber, no vonder, all vinter."

Then, there was the Finlander who went ice fishing.

He brought back 50 pounds of ice.

What was the smart thing the Dane did...who had rented an outhouse to live in?"

He sublet the basement to a Swede.

There's a new Russian drink that is becoming popular, a mixture of vodka and prune juice. It's called a "Pile Driver."

Describe a Polish compass.

It has the letters W E S N on it, plus a small mirror to show who's lost.

A Polish race driver entered the Indianapolis 500. He had to make 75 pit stops...3 for gas and oil and tire changes, and 72 to ask directions.

POLISH SWING

A Bohemian went to see a psychiatrist who began showing him various pictures to test his reaction. First, the Doc held up a picture of an automobile and said "What does this remind you of?" "Sex," answered the Bohemian. "O.K., now what about this?" asked the psychiatrist, holding a picture of a woodland scene. "Sex," answered the Bohunk. "All right, now what does this remind you of?" The doctor was holding a picture of a telephone. "Sex," said our Bohemian. "Boy, you are one sick cookie!" exclaimed the shrink. "ME sick?" screamed the Bohemian, "YOU'RE the one with all the dirty pictures!"

A Swede spent his wedding night sitting on the edge of the bed. He explained to his new bride, "My uncle told me this is supposed to be the most exciting night of my life."

Two Norwegians were sent up in a space capsule. During the flight, one of them went on a scheduled space walk outside the capsule. During the space walk, the door accidentally closed. So the Norwegian inside the capsule suddenly heard a rapping on the door. "Yah, who iss it?" he inquired.

Scotchmen usually work crossword puzzles vertically.

They are too tight to come across.

A Scotchman approached a man who had saved the Scotchman's small son from drowning. "So," said Sandy, "where's the wee laddie's cap?"

Why does it take 3 Polacks to pop popcorn?

One to hold the popper and two to shake the stove.

There's a new Italian sports car on the market called a Mafia. Has a real hood under the hood.

A Swede broke his arm raking leaves. He fell out of a tree.

Then there was the Swede who noticed the sign, "Wet Pavement." So he did.

What do you find on the bottom of cola bottles in Poland?

The inscription "Open other end."

How do you recognize the groom at a Polish wedding?

He's the one with the clean bowling shirt.

There once was a Polish girl who was afraid of flies...until she opened one.

Did you hear about the man who was half Swedish and half Japanese? Every December 7th, he goes out and attacks Pearl Bloomquist.

A Norwegian took his wife to a Doctor. The Doc prescribed that the Norwegian take his wife to the beach for some ocean air. Instead, the thrifty Norwegian stayed at home and fanned her with a herring.

Name two underarm deodorants used by Polish women.

Raid, and Janitor in a Drum.

What do they call the dehydrated Frenchman?

"Pee-Air."

How do you say "Cut the grass" in French?

"Mow ze lawn."

Three Frenchmen were tyring to define the essence of the expression "Savoir Faire."

The first Frenchman said, "When a man come home and find his wife in bed with another man, eef he gently close ze door, zat is Savoir Faire."

The second Frenchman disagreed: "Eef ze man say "Continue," zen close ze door, ZAT is Savoir Faire."

"Au contraire," protested the third Frenchman. "Eef ze husband say "Continue"...and EEF zey continue, ZAT is Savoir Faire."

What is the best way to get the attention of a Polack?

Simply call out: "Attention K Mart Shoppers!"

We heard about a Dane who liked fishing so well that he married a woman with worms.

An Irish politician was approached by a wealthy businessman who apparently needed some favors. The tycoon offered the Irishman a new sports car, but the wily politician declined, explaining his deep sense of public service and innate honesty prevented him from accepting.

"O.K.," said the wealthy businessman. "How about me selling it to you for $10?"

The Irishman thought a moment and responded "Well, in that case, I'll take two."

You've heard of Evel Knievel, the famous stunt driver who broke his back in 8 places leaping over vehicles on his motorcycle. Now, let's have a cheer for Evel Kowalski, the famous Polish stunt driver, who risks his neck by hurtling over 17 motorcycles in his garbage truck.

Know why there are no insane asylums in Norway? If they get loony, they send them to Denmark where they get jobs as school teachers.

At the seashore, an Irishman named Mike had no luck with the ladies. His friend Pat had plenty of women on the string, so he tipped Mike off to stick a potato in his swim trunks. Still no luck. Pat came on the scene and laughed. "Mike, yer sposed ta put the potata down the FRONT!"

Tony, the Italian cook, was serving as lookout on a U.S. merchant ship. Suddenly the captain pointed out to sea and shouted. "Tony, is that a U boat?"

"No, boss, dat's notta my boat," said Tony, "She's a no belong to me!"

A Polish housewife, tired of her husband's stinginess, decided to sell herself on the street. The first night she came back with 50 dollars and 10 cents. Her husband asked, "Who gave you the 10 cents?" "Every one of them," giggled the little woman.

What kind of noise does an Italian make when he hits the ground from a 20 story drop?

"WOP!"

A Norwegian stopped in at a bait shop and inquired as to the cost of worms.

"One dollar for all you need," said the proprieter.

"O.K." answered the Norwegian, "Give me two dollars worth."

How do you say "Brassiere" in German?
"Holzemundkeepsemfromfloppin."

An Italian was being given a test to see if he qualified to become a U.S. citizen. The examiner was trying to explain allegiance to the flag. The Italian did not understand. Finally the examiner asked, "Do you know what flies over the courthouse?" "Sure, boss," said the Italian, "Peedgins."

We heard about a Swede who wanted to be a stud. So he had himself strapped to a snow tire.

An inebriated Pole strolled through an Italian neighborhood. An Italian was barbecuing a chicken on a spit over a charcoal grill. Trying to be helpful, the Polack ran up to the Italian and shouted, "Hey mister...your music stopped and your monkey's on fire!"

A Polack with a frog on his head stepped into the doctor's office. "What seems to be the trouble?" asked the doc. "Well, there's this Polack on my rear end," complained the frog.

That latest earthquake in California was caused, we hear, when they tried to bury a Pole.

The earth rejected the body.

Swede: Ole, stand in front of my car and tell me if my blinkers are working.

Norwegian: "No...yes...no...yes...no...yes...no...yes...

There is one Italian who will go through the rest of his life depressed for the simple reason that, although he is a Cardinal, he can never become Pope. He has the misfortune of being named Giovanni Sicola. Can you imagine? "Pope Sicola"?

A Swede named Joe Johnson showed his co-worker Al Nahum his pet dog with no legs.

"What do you call him?" asked Al.

"Hasn't got a name," answered Joe.

"Why no name?" inquired Nahum.

"Because," said Joe, "If I called him, he couldn't come anyway."

Norm Jackson attended Catholic mass with his Irish friend, Fendig Swern. Jackson was unfamiliar with Catholic ritual, so he tried to follow everything that Swern did. Suddenly, Swern leaned over and whispered, "Jackson, did you let one?" Startled, Jackson whispered back, "No. Was I supposed to?"

An Englishman, Darwin Bell, got his wife a solar clothes dryer for her birthday. A clothes line rope.

Some Norwegians in a mixed neighborhood were discussing their popularity decline. Said one, "I still tink we're popular. I'll ask that Polack over dere. Hey...what do you Polacks tink of us Norvegians?" The Pole thrust up his middle finger, "See," said the Norwegian, "ve're still number vun."

A Pole and a monkey were sent up in a space capsule. The monkey's duties were to push various levers at certain times. The Pole's duties were to feed and water the monkey.

Did you hear about the constipated Polish bookkeeper?

He managed to work things out with a pencil.

What is the largest organization of Polish athletes in the world?

The Fighting Irish of Notre Dame.

3 most dangerous people in the world:

An Irishman with a bottle of whiskey

A merchant with a box of matches

A Norwegian with a little education.

Why don't Italians have pimples?

Because they'd slide right off.

We know a German who's so dumb he thinks a "crotch" is the place Lawrence Welk parks his Dotch.

A Swede began singing a hymn he learned at church. His fellow workers asked the name of it, and what it was about. He explained it was about a cross-eyed bear named Gladly. Someone checked with the preacher and found the hymn to be "Gladly the Cross I'd Bear."

An Irishman had been on a little party and after a few flagons of ale attempted to drive home. Leaning out of his car window, he hailed a passing policeman. "Shay, offisher," he complained, "somebody has stole me steering wheel, gearshift, clutch and brakes." The cop quickly surmised that the potted Irishman had climbed into the back seat.

A Norwegian showed up at work with a black eye. He explained it as being caused by "Seenus trouble."

"No, no," said one of his co-workers. "It's called "SINUS TROUBLE."

"Vell, all I know," said the Norwegian, "is that I vas out vid a married voman and her husband seen us."

A Swede in Minneapolis moved his house back 50 feet to take up the slack in his clothes line.

How can it be proved that Adam was a Pole?

Who else would stand beside a naked woman and just eat an apple?

Maybe you heard about the Swede who got stranded on an escalator during a power outage.

Why are Polish mothers so strong?

From raising dumb-bells.

Why were wheelbarrows invented?

To teach the Irish to walk on their hind legs.

What is the smallest building in the world?

The Polish Hall of Fame.

A Polish student in school, explaining "heredity" to his teacher: "It means that if your parents didn't have any children, chances are you won't have any either."

There once was a Norwegian who, in a rage, flung himself upon the floor. And missed.

On a stormy night, a farmer was wakened by a pounding at the door. It was a German asking for shelter. The farmer said the house was crowded so he'd be better off to sleep in the barn with the pigs. Thirty minutes later, the German was unable to tolerate the atmosphere in the barn and asked to come in the house. Shortly, a Frenchman knocked at the door and was told the same thing. Soon, the Frenchman was knocking, begging to stay in the house. Then, a Norwegian rapped at the door and was sent to the barn for shelter. Ten minutes later, the pigs all ran out of the barn, heading for the house.

Swedish Girl: "Have you ever been picked up by the fuzz?"

Norwegian Girl: "No, but I'll bet it hurts."

We know an Irishman who lived the life of Riley...until one week Riley came home early.

There once was a Swedish butcher who backed into the meat grinder and got a little behind in his work.

The Irishman was being executed and as they adjusted the noose, he burst into laughter. When the executioner asked the reason for his merriment, the condemned man chuckled, "The joke is on you...it wasn't me that did the crime."

The Pole ordered a pizza and was asked whether he wanted it cut in four or eight pieces. "Better cut it in four," he said, "I'm not hungry enough to eat eight pieces."

Two Swedes opened a bank. After loaning out all the money, they skipped town.

Customer: "Do you have the book, 'The Smart Norwegian?'

Bookstore Clerk: "Yes. It's in the fiction department."

A Pole was bragging about his girl friend, saying that her family was in Iron and Steel. His friends found out that the mother ironed while the father would steal.

Slogan of the Women's libbers in Ireland: "Erin go bra-less."

Describe Polish cough medicine: A bottle of Castor oil. Two spoonfuls and you don't DARE cough.

Why are there so few suicides in Polish neighborhoods?

It's hard to get hurt jumping out of basement windows.

Here is a supposed interview with Lawrence Welk, whose German accent belies the fact he was born and raised in North Dakota.

Interviewer: "Mr. Welk . . . what is your opinion on violence?

Welk: "Next to da accordion, I like da violence da best."

An Italian gambler died and his funeral was attended by a number of his gambling cronies. As the minister intoned the eulogy, he concluded by saying, "Tony is not dead . . . he only sleeps." From the back of the chapel came a raspy voice, "I've got Five G's that says he ain't wakin' up."

A sweet little old Irish nun was standing at a bus stop on a hot day when she appeared to be swooning from the heat. A kindly young policeman came to her rescue and hurried her into the corner tavern where he hoped to revive her with a touch of spirits.

"Sister, perhaps I'd better get you a bit of brandy to bring you around," said the cop. "That would be fine," said the Sister, "and would you have it put in a paper cup?"

The policeman stepped up to the bartender and said, "A double Manhattan please, and would you kindly put it in a paper cup?"

The bartender raised his head and snorted, "Is that little nun in here again?"

A Polack who had become aware of first aid measures came across a friend who had been injured and was bleeding from a cut lip. So the Polack put a tourniquet around the victim's neck to stop the bleeding.

There was a Swede so lazy that he married a pregnant woman.

We heard of a Polack who painted his garbage cans orange and black so he could fool his kids into thinking they were being taken to the A & W.

"Polish military salute"

A Polish girl walked down the street with a pig under her arm. A drunk noticed the scene and queried, "Shay . . . where didja get the pig?"

Pig: "I won her in a raffle."

Why did they quit circumsizing Irishmen?

--Because they found they were throwing away the best part.

Why do flies have wings?

So they can beat the Norwegians to the garbage cans.

What does a Swede say when he picks his nose?

Grace.

What is the most dangerous job in Poland?

Riding shotgun on the garbage truck.

How do you say "Refrigerator" in Italian?

"Ice-a-box."

What do Italians call Canada?

"Upper U.S."

What do they call Alaska?

"Way Upper U.S."

How do Italians say "Large fog?"

"Big-a-mist."

What do the Italians call an astronaut?

"Specimen."

What do you get when you cross a Polack with a Jew?

A janitor who owns the building.

Who pumped the 4 bullets into Mussolini when he was assassinated?

100 Italian sharpshooters.

Why do Italian boats have the letters A.M.B. on the bow?

A.M.B. stands for "Atsa my boat."

There's a new Polish birth control method called "Sulfa Denial."

It's a derivative of No-acetol.

What is a Polish no-hitter?

That's a Polish wedding before the priest leaves.

Then the story about the Italian who was so simple he thought Vat 69 was the Pope's phone number.

Back in the days when milk was delivered by a horse and wagon, a German hollered at the milkman, "Hey mister . . . you won't get home tonight . . . your horse just ran out of gas."

A Polish fox became caught in a trap. It chewed off three of its feet only to find out it was still caught.

How do you identify the bride at a Polish wedding?

She's the one with the braided armpits.

During the North African campaign in WW II, one of the Lieutenants volunteered to go into the desert on a camel to scout the location of Rommel's army. After two days, back at the camp the Polish radio operator brought the Commander a radio message from the Lieutenant, "Rommel captured." The following day, the exhausted Lieutenant staggered into camp. The Commander showed him the radio message the Polack had handed him. "No, no," gasped the Lieutenant . . . "my message said 'Camel ruptured!' "

Who was Alexander Graham Kalezewski?

The first telephone Pole

Ordinarily "TGIF" means "Thank goodness it's Friday." Why do Norwegians have "TGIF" printed on their shoes?
It means "Toes go in first."

How do you break a Norwegian's finger?

Punch him in the nose.

What is a big awkward animal with a trunk?

A Polack on vacation.

What is the Norwegian national anthem?

"Shoo Fly Don't Bother Me."

Stanley Zalinski was age 25 but not very sophisticated about dating girls. One night he was out with Sophie, took her to a movie, bought her a sack of buttered popcorn and a bottle of pop. Afterward, Sophie suggested they go somewhere and park. After finding a suitably dark location, Sophie asked, "Stanley, how would you like to go in the back seat?"

"Heck no," exclaimed Stanley, "I want to stay up here with you."

What is the sign posted at the entrance of the city dump?

"Polish Country Club."

How can you spot the Pole in a motorcycle gang?

He's got the cycle with the training wheels.

An old Irish lady approached a Pole visiting in Ireland, asking if he would locate her son, John Dunne, who had left for America and hadn't written as promised. When the Pole reached New York, he spied a sign, "Dun & Bradstreet." Sure that he'd found his man, the Pole walked in and asked if they had a "John". "Yes," down the hall said the secretary. The Pole walked in the restroom and saw a man standing at a urinal. "Are you Dunne?" he asked. "Yes, I'm done," said the man." "Well," said the Pole, "Why don't you write your Mother in Ireland."

Why do Polacks have flat heads and round shoulders?

When you ask them a question, they go like this.

And when you tell them the answer, they go like this.

What is a Russian shishkabob?

A flaming arrow through a garbage can.

At the local vinegar works, the Irish played the Italians a game of football. When the 5 o'clock whistle blew, the Irishmen went home. Four plays later, the Italians scored a touchdown.

What is a Polack called who chases garbage trucks?

"A galloping gourmet."

Polish seven course meal: A Polish sausage and a six pack of beer.

We heard of a German who stayed up all night studying for his urine test.

A Swede received his draft notice and was told to bring a urine sample to the Selective Service Headquarters. Figuring on outfoxing the draft board, the Swede filled a bottle with urine from his father, girl friend, and dog, plus some of his own. After turning in the sample, the Swede waited for about a half hour. The lab technician came out to tell him: "According to our lab tests, your father has diabetes, your girl friend is pregnant, your dog is in heat, and YOU'RE in the Army."

A Scotchman got involved in a legal matter. That night he paid a call on his girl friend and asked if she'd care to see his subpoena. She slapped his face.

The Polack's little boy had just started going to school. One night the mother asked, "Casimir, how much is 4 plus 4?" To which the little fellow replied "Seven." "The kid's got brains," exclaimed the proud father, "he only missed it by three."

The Swede walked into a lumber yard and asked if they could make him a box 1 inch wide by 50 feet long. The puzzled lumber man, upon inquiry, found that the Swede was planning to ship a garden hose that he'd borrowed from a neighbor who had moved to California.

The Scotchman's little boy came home from school and announced: "Papa . . . I need an encyclopedia for school."

Grumbled the Scotchman, "Nothing doing, Laddy, ye kin walk to school like I did when I was a lad."

Why do they bury Polacks with their rear ends sticking out of the ground?

So they can be used for bicycle racks.

How do you make a Hungarian omelet?
First . . . you steal a dozen eggs . . . .

An Irishman named Leevada Moore showed up where he worked explaining he had "MOM" tattooed on his stomach. "Why not on your chest?" inquired his friend, Randy Brown. "Because," said Moore, I got more room on my stomach. And besides, the "O" is free."

"Gunner" Witowski joined the Navy and was personally responsible for destroying 15 Japanese planes. As fate would have it, this was in 1971.

Teacher: "Stash, how do you spell 'Mississippi'?"
Polish Kid: "Which one? The river or the state?"

A Polish lady stood weeping at the gates of the cemetery. A passerby tried to comfort her. She sobbed, "I've got a daughter lying out in that cemetery. Sometimes I almost wish she was dead."

Recently we heard about a Polish bookkeeper who absconded with the Accounts Payable.

Customer in a Polish restaurant: "Waiter . . . what is that fly doing in my soup?"
Polish Waiter: "Hmmm . . . I believe the backstroke."

A Bohemian motorist was stopped by a cop, doing 100 miles an hour. "What's your hurry," asked the cop. "My brakes gave out," explained the Bohemian, "So I was trying to hurry home before I had an accident."

Q. Where do the Swedes keep their armies?
A. Up their sleevies.

How do Poles spell "farm?"
"E-I-E-I-O"

Did you hear about the Swedish girl who had a wooden baby?
Seems she got nailed by a carpenter.

What is it that's "Wet and Wild?"
An Irishman with a stuck zipper.